T-Shirt
F·U·N

PETRA BOASE

LORENZ BOOKS

LONDON • NEW YORK • SYDNEY • BATH

This edition first published in the UK in 1997 by Lorenz Books

Lorenz Books is an imprint of Anness Publishing Limited,
Hermes House, 88-89 Blackfriars Road, London SE1 8HA

This edition published in Canada by Raincoast Books,
8680 Cambie Street, Vancouver, British Columbia VP6 6M9

ISBN 1 85967 508 5

A CIP catalogue record for this book is available from the British Library.

Publisher: Joanna Lorenz
Managing Editor, Children's Books: Sue Grabham
Editor: Lyn Coutts
Photographer: John Freeman
Designer: Caroline Grimshaw

Printed and bound in China

1 3 5 7 9 10 8 6 4 2

Introduction

Decorating T-shirts with fabric paints, threads and material is fun and very easy to do. In no time at all you will be creating stylish and wacky T-shirts for yourself, friends and family.

This book shows you how to prepare T-shirts as well as how to use different types of fabric paints to achieve brilliant effects. It is also bursting with ideas. There are T-shirt designs for sports fans, disco dancers and animal lovers. There are even T-shirt designs for fancy-dress parties. Most of the projects are simple to do. Others are more difficult and use special techniques.

Once you have painted your first T-shirt, there will be no stopping you. You will be painting sweatshirts, leggings and even fabrics for your bedroom. So get to it and have fun!

Petra Boase

Contents

GETTING STARTED

T-SHIRT FUN

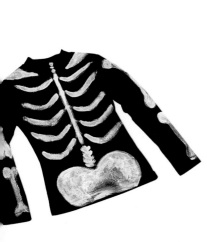

Materials

CHALK FABRIC MARKER
This is a special white chalk that is used for drawing outlines on to dark coloured T-shirts.

EMBROIDERY NEEDLE
The large eye in this needle makes it easy to thread with embroidery thread.

EMBROIDERY THREAD
A strong, thick thread that is used for decorative stitching. It comes in lots of bright colours.

FABRIC GLUE
This glue will stick pieces of fabric together. Always use a special brush for applying fabric glue.

FABRIC MARKER PEN
A fabric marker pen looks like a normal felt tip pen but it is designed to be used on fabric.

FABRIC PAINT
Fabric paint is applied on to fabric and will not wash out. Always read the instructions on the container before using it.

FELT
Felt is easy to cut and will not fray. It can be bought in fabric or hobby shops.

FLUORESCENT FABRIC PAINT
Under ultra violet light, this paint will glow. It comes in many bright colours.

GLITTER
This is special glitter that can be fixed to fabric with fabric glue. It is very fine, so use it carefully.

GLITTER FABRIC PAINT
This sparkly fabric paint comes in a tube or squeezy container. Always follow the instructions on the packaging.

HAIRDRYER
You will need a hairdryer with a low heat setting to dry puffa fabric paint.

HAIR CLIPS
To complete one of the projects, you will need two clip-on plastic hair grips.

NEWSPAPER
To protect your work surface, cover it with newspaper.

PAINTBRUSHES
You will need fine, medium and thick paintbrushes. Always wash the brushes before changing fabric paint colours.

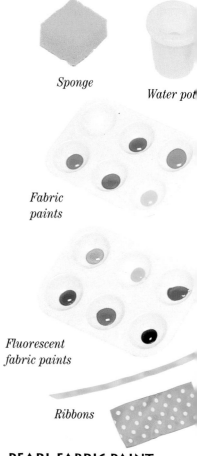

Sponge

Water pot

Fabric paints

Fluorescent fabric paints

Ribbons

PEARL FABRIC PAINT
This fabric paint dries with a special sheen. It comes in a squeezy container.

PUFFA FABRIC PAINT
When dried with a hairdryer, this paint puffs up. It comes in a squeezy container. Always follow the manufacturer's instructions when using puffa paint.

Puffa
fabric paint

Pearl
fabric paint

Glitter
fabric paint

Stiff card

Embroidery
needle

Knitting
wool

Embroidery
thread

Thick paintbrush

Hair clips

Sewing needle
and thread

Tracing paper

Medium paintbrush

Scissors

Ruler

Fine paintbrush

Plate

Newspaper

Fabric marker pen

Sequins

Sticky back hook
and loop dots

Sewing
pins

Pencil

T-shirt

Felt

Glitter

Fabric glue
and brush

Chalk fabric
marker

Paper

Hairdryer

SEQUINS
These colourful shiny shapes are
fixed to fabric with fabric glue.

SPONGE
You can buy an inexpensive
sponge from a chemist shop.
A sponge dipped in fabric paint
and pressed on to fabric makes
an interesting texture. A sponge
is also used in stencilling.

STICKY BACK HOOK AND
LOOP DOTS
These dots stick to each other
when pressed together. Remove
the backing to fix them to fabric.

STIFF CARD
Pieces of card are inserted into
a T-shirt to stop fabric paint
seeping through. Use card to
make stencils and templates.

TRACING PAPER
This is special paper that you
can see through. It is used to
trace templates and stencils. You
can buy it in stationery shops.

T-SHIRT
For the projects in this book you
will need cotton T-shirts. There
are designs for short and long
sleeved styles.

7

Preparing the T-shirt

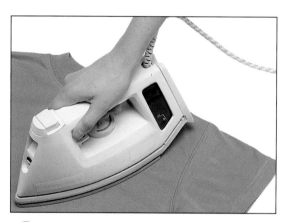

1 If you are using a new T-shirt, it is a good idea to wash and rinse it to remove excess dye. When the T-shirt is dry, ask an adult to iron it to smooth out creases.

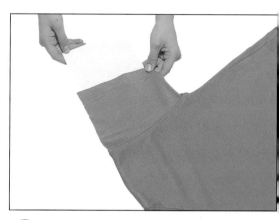

2 To stop fabric paint seeping through the T-shirt, insert pieces of stiff card into the body and sleeves. The pieces of card should fit snugly into position.

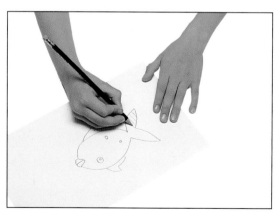

3 Draw roughs of your design on a piece of paper before drawing it on the T-shirt. Fabric marker pen, like fabric paints, cannot be washed out.

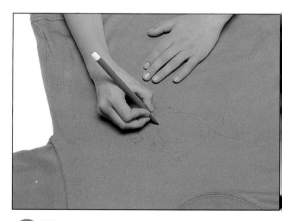

4 When you are happy with your design, draw it on to the T-shirt. Use a fabric marker pen on light coloured T-shirts. For dark T-shirts, use a chalk fabric marker.

Painting Tips

1 If you only have a few fabric paints, you can mix them together to make other colours. For example, yellow + blue = green, yellow + red = orange, red + blue = purple.

2 If you need a large quantity of a colour, it is best to mix it in a water pot or small bowl. Add water to your fabric paints to make them go further.

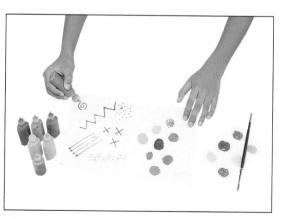

3 Before painting the T-shirt, try out the techniques and the colours on a piece of fabric. This is especially important when using fabric paints in squeezy containers.

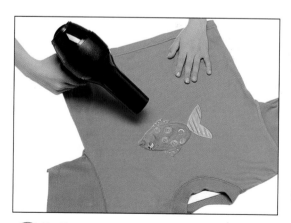

4 Puffa paint only puffs up when it is dried with a hairdryer, set on low heat. Before drying other fabric paints with a hairdryer, check the instructions on the paint container.

Tracing a Template

1 Place a sheet of tracing paper over the outline. Use masking tape to keep the tracing paper in position. Draw over the outline with a dark lead pencil.

2 Remove the tracing paper and turn it face down on to a sheet of paper. Use the lead pencil to draw lots of fine lines over the back of the traced outline.

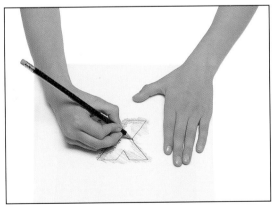

3 Place the tracing paper with the traced outline face up on to a piece of thin card. Draw over the outline. The outline will be transferred on to the card.

4 To make the template, cut out the outline with a pair of scissors. Place the template on to the T-shirt and draw around it. Keep the template so that it can be used again.

Templates

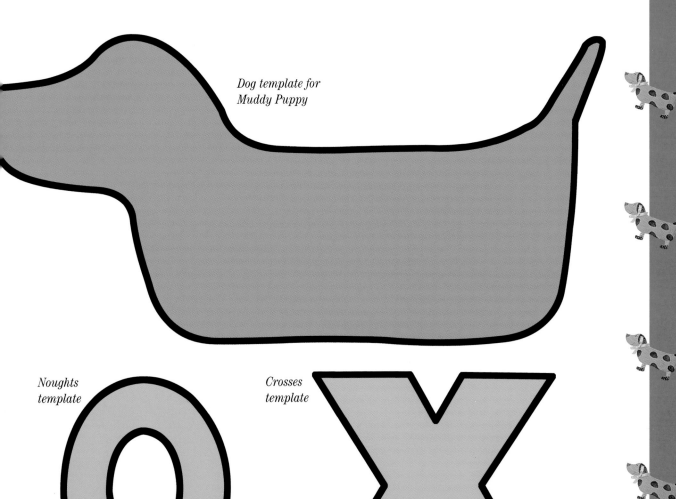

Dog template for Muddy Puppy

Noughts template

Crosses template

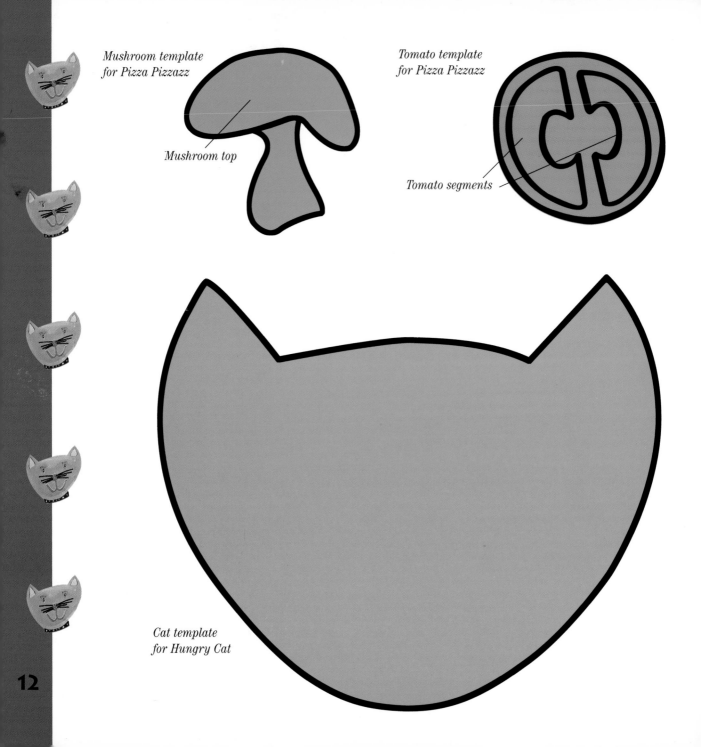

Mushroom template
for Pizza Pizzazz

Mushroom top

Tomato template
for Pizza Pizzazz

Tomato segments

Cat template
for Hungry Cat

Making a Stencil

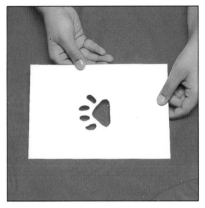

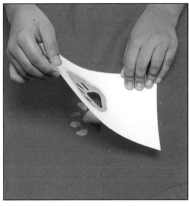

1 Follow steps 1 to 3 on page 10 to make a tracing of the outline. Use scissors to snip into the middle of the outline. Cut out the stencil following the outline.

2 Place the stencil on to the T-shirt. Lightly press a dry sponge into fabric paint. Then dab the sponge on to the stencil.

3 Carefully lift the stencil off the T-shirt. Before using it again, check that there are no blobs of paint on the back.

STENCILS

Fish skeleton stencil for Hungry Cat

Paws stencil for Muddy Puppy

13

Tooty Fruity

The fruit on this T-shirt looks good enough to eat! To make the fruit look realistic, paint areas of shadow and light. Add texture with dots of pearl fabric paint and felt leaves.

YOU WILL NEED

Large sheet of card
Short sleeved T-shirt
Fabric marker pen
Pot of water
Fabric paint (yellow, red, pink, crimson)
Thick paintbrush
Pearl fabric paint (yellow, pink)
Green felt
Scissors
Fabric glue and brush

14

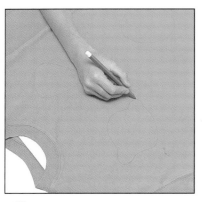

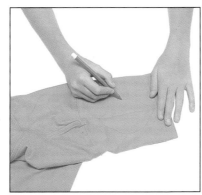

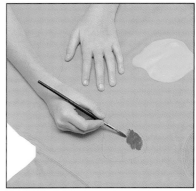

1 Insert a piece of card inside the body of the T-shirt. Use the fabric marker pen to draw the outlines of a lemon, strawberry, raspberry and orange on to the front of the T-shirt.

2 Lay one sleeve out flat so that the seam is on the bottom. Insert a piece of card into the sleeve. Use the fabric marker pen to draw a piece of fruit on to the sleeve. Repeat on the other sleeve.

3 Use the thick brush to paint the fruit on the front of the T-shirt with fabric paint. To make orange, mix together red and yellow. Allow the fabric paint to dry before painting the fruit on to the sleeves.

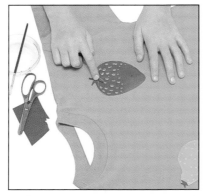

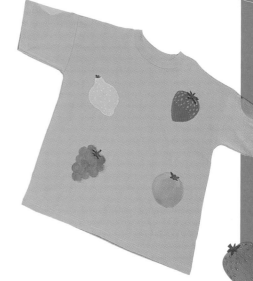

4 To add texture to the orange, strawberry and lemon, make dots using yellow and pink pearl fabric paint. Allow to dry before doing the same to the pieces of fruit on the sleeves.

5 Use the fabric marker pen to draw the outlines of leaves on to the green felt. Cut out the leaves and glue them on to the fruit with fabric glue. Allow to dry before trying on your Tooty Fruity T-shirt.

Muddy Puppy

Oh, no! Someone has let the puppy walk all over this T-shirt with its muddy paws! Surely such a naughty puppy does not deserve to be given a big, juicy bone! To stop the puppy covering everything with mud, it has been given a fancy pair of socks to wear.

YOU WILL NEED
2 sheets of card
Short sleeved T-shirt
Pencil
Tracing paper
Scissors
Fabric marker pen
Pot of water
Fabric paint (brown, black, white,
*   turquoise, red, pale blue, yellow)*
Fine and thick paintbrushes
Narrow yellow ribbon
Fabric glue and brush
Sponge

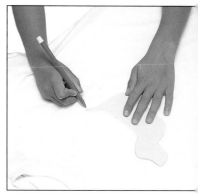

1 Insert pieces of card inside the body and sleeves of the T-shirt. Trace the template for the dog on page 11. Place the template on to the front of the T-shirt. Draw around it using the fabric marker pen.

2 Paint the dog brown using the thick brush. If you do not have brown paint, make some by mixing together blue, red and yellow. Make light and dark shades of brown by adding white or black. Allow to dry before starting the next step.

16

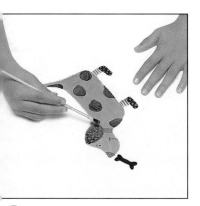

3 Use the fine brush to paint black spots on to the body. Continue using the black to paint the ear, tail, shoes and bone. Add features to the face and decorate the socks and shoes. Paint a collar.

4 Allow the paint to dry before starting this step. Tie the piece of ribbon into a small bow. Trim the ends. Fix the bow on to the collar with fabric glue. Hold the bow in position until the glue is dry.

5 Trace the paw print stencil on page 13. Cut out the stencil, as shown. Turn the T-shirt over so that the back is facing you. Make sure that the pieces of card are still in position inside the T-shirt.

6 Place the stencil on to the T-shirt. Hold it in position and use a sponge to dab light and dark brown fabric paint on to the stencil. Lift off the stencil. Repeat until the back of the T-shirt is covered with muddy paw prints.

Crazy Spiral

The Crazy Spiral T-shirt is simple to do if you are new to fabric painting. Draw the outline of the spiral as large as you can to make it easy to paint and to decorate. You can add smaller spirals to the design or paint a spiral on to the back of your T-shirt, too.

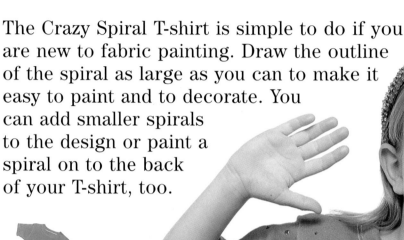

YOU WILL NEED

Large sheet of card
Short sleeved T-shirt
Fabric marker pen
Pot of water
Fabric paint (black, orange, yellow,
 light blue, green)
Fine, medium and thick paintbrushes
Pearl fabric paint (yellow,
 orange, purple)
Glitter fabric paint (green, purple)

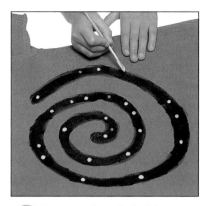

1 Insert pieces of card inside the body and sleeves of the T-shirt. Use the fabric marker pen to draw a large curly spiral on to the front of the T-shirt.

2 Paint the spiral with black fabric paint using the thick brush. Allow the paint to dry thoroughly before starting the next step.

3 Decorate the spiral with orange, yellow, light blue and green dots of fabric paint. Do this using the medium brush. Allow the paint to dry thoroughly.

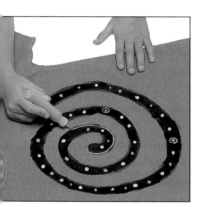

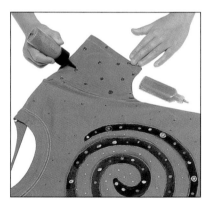

4 Draw circles around some of the dots using yellow pearl fabric paint. Go around the outline of the spiral with orange and purple pearl fabric paint. Leave the paint to dry.

5 Make dots of yellow pearl fabric paint inside the spiral. Use glitter fabric paint to cover the front of the T-shirt with green dots. To finish, dot the sleeves with purple glitter fabric paint.

Swirly Spots and Dots

This is the perfect T-shirt to wear when you are out with your friends for a day of madcap adventures. The design is very simple to draw and you can use as many or as few colours as you like. It is important that the fabric paint is dry before you start decorating the circles with puffa and glitter fabric paints.

YOU WILL NEED
Large sheet of card
Short sleeved T-shirt
Fabric marker pen
Pot of water
Medium paintbrush

Fabric paint (red, black,
   pink, blue, white)
Puffa fabric paint (purple,
   red, yellow, orange, blue)
Hairdryer
Glitter fabric paint (silver)

1 Insert pieces of card inside the body and sleeves of the T-shirt. Use the fabric marker pen to draw large circles on to the front of the T-shirt. Draw circles on to sleeves as well.

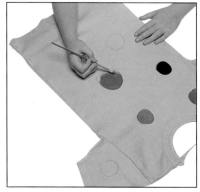

2 Use the medium brush to paint the circles different colours. Do not forget to wash the brush when changing colours. Allow the fabric paint to dry thoroughly before starting the next step.

3 Use purple, red, yellow, orange and blue puffa fabric paint to decorate some of the circles with swirls, lines, dots and spots. To make the puffa fabric paint puff up, dry it with the hairdryer.

*When using puffa or glitter fabric
paints in squeezy containers,
always keep the nozzle moving
smoothly and evenly over your
design. If you let the nozzle stay
in one place for too long, the
paint will form blobs.*

④ To make your T-shirt even
more dazzling, decorate the
remaining circles with silver glitter
fabric paint. To finish, add glitter
fabric paint to those circles already
decorated with puffa fabric paint.

Bug Collector

Aargh! Do not look now but there are spiders and insects crawling all over you. The Bug Collector T-shirt is not for the squeamish – it is for the enthusiastic mini-beast collector who really wants to bug his friends and family. You can invent your own creatures, or better still, copy them from real life!

YOU WILL NEED

Large sheet of card
Long sleeved T-shirt
Fabric marker pen
Pot of water
Fabric paint (black, red)

Fine and medium
   paintbrushes
Black fabric paint or
   pearl fabric paint in
   squeezy containers

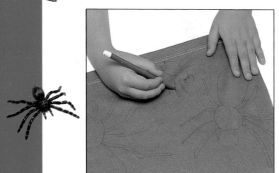

1 Insert pieces of card inside the body and sleeves of the T-shirt. Use the fabric marker pen to draw three large spiders on to the front of the T-shirt. Draw two or three spiders on to each sleeve.

2 Use the medium brush and black fabric paint to paint the spiders' heads, bodies and fangs. To paint the black jointed legs, use the fine brush. Wash the brush before painting the spiders' eyes red.

3 Dip a finger into black fabric paint and press it on to the T-shirt to make the body and head of a small insect. Repeat until you have covered the front of the T-shirt with mini-beasts. Allow to dry.

22

HANDY HINT

To make repeated designs, like the small spiders, you could make a stamp with a halved potato. Etch the shape into a cut surface of the potato with a blunt pencil. Ask an adult to cut away the potato from around the shape with a sharp knife. Dip the stamp into fabric paint and press it on to the T-shirt.

4 To paint legs on the small bugs, use black fabric paint or pearl fabric paint in squeezy containers. Allow the paint to dry. If you like, you can paint more bugs on to the back of the T-shirt.

23

Cactus Flower

This cactus has been painted on to a yellow T-shirt because cacti grow in deserts. Even though rain rarely falls in the desert, a cactus can live for over 100 years! It has prickly spines so that it does not lose moisture and to stop animals eating its juicy trunk. When it does rain, the cactus bursts into flower.

YOU WILL NEED

Large sheet of card
Scissors
Short sleeved T-shirt
Fabric marker pen
Pot of water
Medium paintbrush

Fabric paint (red, blue, pink, dark and light green, yellow)
Green embroidery thread
Embroidery needle

1 Insert pieces of card into the body and sleeves of the T-shirt. Use the fabric marker pen to draw a flowering cactus and plant pot on the front of the T-shirt. Draw a decorative pattern around the pot.

2 Draw zigzag patterns along the bottom of the T-shirt, the edges of the sleeves and around the collar with the marker pen. Use the medium brush to paint the pattern with red and blue fabric paint.

3 Paint the pot red and the flower pink, then paint the border around the pot blue. Roughly paint the cactus with light and dark green fabric paint. To make light green, add yellow to dark green.

24

4 Allow the fabric paint to dry. Thread the needle with the thread. Tie a knot at the end. Push the needle and thread in and out of the front of the T-shirt to sew large stitches on to the cactus. These are the cactus's prickly spikes. Secure the thread with a knot to finish.

HANDY HINT
Before decorating the back of a T-shirt, the front must be dry. You can speed up the drying by using a hairdryer but before doing so, check the instructions on the fabric paint containers. When you turn the T-shirt over, make sure that the pieces of card are still in position.

Space Trekker

This T-shirt goes where no other T-shirt has gone before. Its fluorescent yellow after-burners will be seen by alien beings in all the far-flung galaxies. But all Space Trekkers should make sure that they know how to get back to Planet Earth!

YOU WILL NEED

Large sheet of card
Dark, short sleeved T-shirt
Chalk fabric marker
Pot of water
Fabric paint (dark blue, light blue, black, red, fluorescent yellow, silver)
Medium and thick paintbrushes
Pearl fabric paint (red)

26

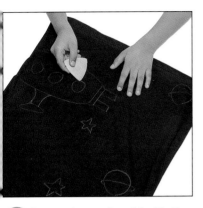

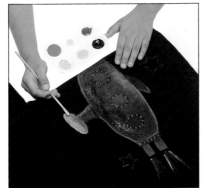

1 Insert pieces of card inside the body and sleeves of the T-shirt. Use the chalk fabric marker to draw the outlines of planets, stars and a rocket. Draw only the end of the rocket and its thrusters on to the front of the T-shirt.

2 Use the medium and thick brushes to paint the rocket with dark blue, light blue, black and red fabric paint. Use fluorescent yellow fabric paint for rivets and the glow of the after-burners. Paint the top of the rocket with silver fabric paint.

3 Paint the stars with silver fabric paint. Use plain and fluorescent fabric paints for the planets. When the paint is dry, make a ring around each planet with red pearl fabric paint. Use the pearl fabric paint to add extra details to the rocket.

4 To make galaxies of stars, dip the thick brush in yellow fluorescent fabric paint and then flick the brush at the T-shirt. Droplets of paint will scatter all over it. Repeat until the T-shirt is aglow with dazzling stars. Allow the paint to dry before starting the next step.

5 Turn the T-shirt over, making sure that the pieces of card are still in position. Use the chalk fabric marker to draw the front of the rocket so that it lines up with the section on the front. Paint and decorate the rocket and the galaxy of stars as before.

Sea Life Fantasy

When you look at this T-shirt you can almost smell the salty air, hear the crash of the waves and see the schools of brightly coloured fish darting backward and forward in a pale blue ocean. In this design there are only two species of marine life, but you could also add some crabs, shells, coral and bright green fronds of seaweed.

YOU WILL NEED
Large sheet of card
Short sleeved blue T-shirt
Fabric marker pen
Pot of water
Fabric paint (light blue, dark blue, yellow, pink, red, black)
Fine and thick paintbrushes

1 Insert the piece of card inside the body of the T-shirt. Use the fabric marker pen to draw the outlines of the fish, starfish and waves on to the front of the T-shirt.

2 Paint the waves with light and dark blue fabric paint using the thick brush. Do not worry if the paint does not go on smoothly – an uneven texture will look more realistic.

3 Paint the fish in shades of blue, green, pink and red. The green can be made by mixing yellow and blue. Use the fine brush to paint the lips and eyes. Paint black bubbles coming from their mouths. Mix red and yellow to make orange. Paint the starfish with the orange paint.

4 Allow the fabric paint to dry thoroughly. Turn the T-shirt over, making sure that the piece of card is still in position. Use the fabric marker pen to draw another fish on to the back of the T-shirt. Continue the pattern of the waves.

5 Use the thick brush to paint the waves with light and dark blue fabric paint. Wash the brush before painting the fish pink with yellow spots. Paint features on to the fish's face and bubbles coming from its mouth.

Basketaller

If you can slam dunk and dribble, then this is the T-shirt design for you. Why not get together with some friends to make a basketball team? You can have a different number each and choose your own team colours.

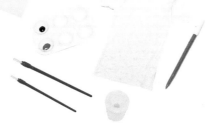

YOU WILL NEED

Large sheet of card
Short sleeved T-shirt
Fabric marker pen
Pot of water
Fabric paint (red, black)
Medium and thick paintbrushes

1 Insert pieces of card inside the body and sleeves of the T-shirt. Use the fabric marker pen to draw the outline of the number 7 on to the front. Draw two bands along the edge of each sleeve front.

2 Use the thick brush to fill in the outline of the number with red fabric paint. Try to apply the paint evenly and smoothly. Allow the paint to dry thoroughly before starting the next step.

3 Paint a narrow line around the number using the medium brush and black fabric paint. You can change these colours to match your favourite team if you like. Allow the paint to dry.

HANDY HINT

Use a ruler to help you make the outlines for the number and the bands straight.

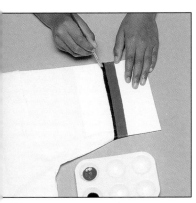

4 Wash the thick brush and use it to fill in the bottom outline on each sleeve with red fabric paint. When the fabric paint is dry, use the medium brush to paint the narrower black line.

5 Paint the ribbing around the neck of the T-shirt with black fabric paint. When dry, use the medium brush to paint the narrow red line. Allow to dry. Turn over the T-shirt and repeat steps 1 to 5.

Hawaiian Dancer

Aloha! Welcome to a tropical luau. Luau is the Hawaiian word for party and the traditional dress for a luau dancer is a grass skirt with a lei of flowers around her neck. Wear some flowers in your hair and around your wrist and you are ready to do the hula dance.

YOU WILL NEED

Large sheet of card
Long, sleeveless, flesh-coloured
*   T-shirt*
Fabric marker pen
Pot of water
Fabric paint (yellow, pink, orange,
*   red, white, green)*
Fine and thick paintbrushes

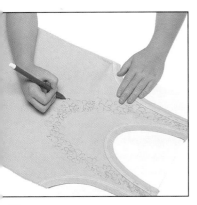

1. Insert a piece of card inside the body of the T-shirt. Use the fabric marker pen to draw the outline of the lei of flowers, navel and grass skirt on to the front of the T-shirt.

2. Use the fine brush to paint the lei of yellow, pink, orange and red flowers. Add white to these colours to make lighter shades. Allow the paint to dry.

3. To paint the grass skirt, use the thick brush and different shades of green fabric paint. You can make different shades of green by adding yellow or white.

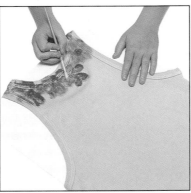

4. To make the navel, use the fine brush and pink fabric paint. Allow the fabric paint to dry. Turn the T-shirt over, making sure that the piece of card is still in position.

5. Use the fabric marker pen to draw the outline of the lei of flowers and skirt. Paint these as before. When the paint has dried, you are ready to hula!

Bones, the Skeleton

This spooky T-shirt is perfect for a Halloween fancy dress party. All you need to complete your nightmare outfit is a tight-fitting black cap, black leggings and a pair of black gloves. To make up your face as a skull, use white face paint or talcum powder and black eye shadow.

YOU WILL NEED

Large sheet of card
Long sleeved black T-shirt
Chalk fabric marker

Pot of water
Fabric paint (white)
Thick paintbrush

1 Insert pieces of card inside the body and sleeves of the T-shirt. Use the chalk fabric marker to draw the outlines of the shoulder blades, rib cage, spine and hips.

2 Use the chalk fabric marker to draw the outlines of the upper and lower arm bones on to the front of both sleeves. These bones should be long and thick.

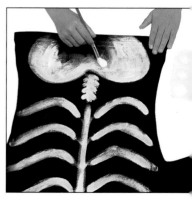

3 Use the thick brush to paint the bones on to the front of the T-shirt with white fabric paint. To make them really white, do two coats. Allow the paint to dry between coats.

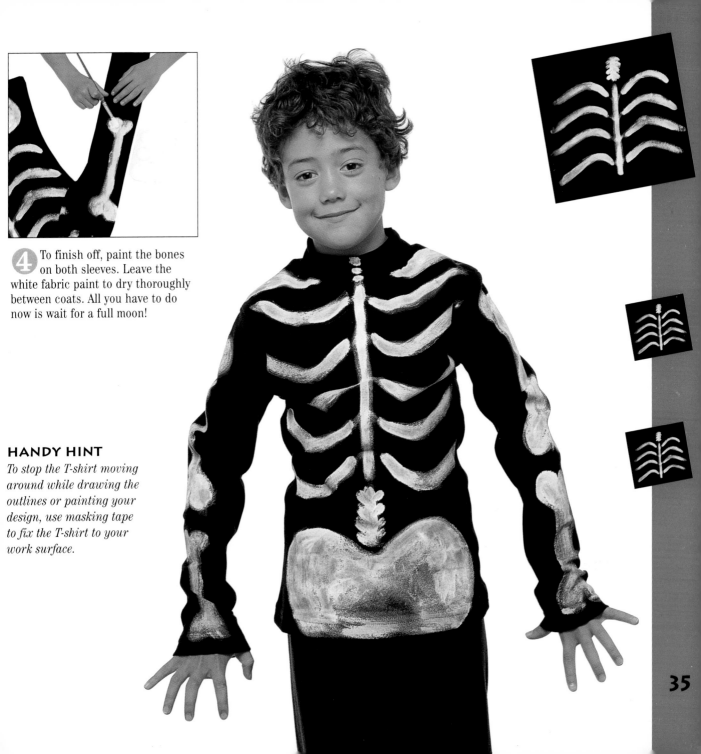

4 To finish off, paint the bones on both sleeves. Leave the white fabric paint to dry thoroughly between coats. All you have to do now is wait for a full moon!

HANDY HINT
To stop the T-shirt moving around while drawing the outlines or painting your design, use masking tape to fix the T-shirt to your work surface.

Pockets of Fun

The Pockets of Fun T-shirt means that you will no longer lose or leave at home all your favourite bits and bobs. You can even use one of the pockets for keeping your pocket money safe! Why not make a matching T-shirt as a present for your best friend?

YOU WILL NEED

Scissors
Orange, mauve, green and blue felt
Fabric glue and brush
Short sleeved T-shirt
Sewing pins
Embroidery needle
Yellow, orange and green embroidery thread
Fabric marker pen
Large sheet of card
Pot of water
Fabric paint (light blue, pink, yellow, orange, red, gold)
Medium paintbrush

36

① Cut three pockets and three decorative strips from the orange, mauve, green and blue felt. The strips must be long enough to fit along the top edge of each pocket. Glue a strip on to the top of each pocket with fabric glue.

② Position the pockets along the bottom of the T-shirt with pins. Thread the needle with embroidery thread and tie a knot in the end. Use thread that is a different colour from the pocket. Sew the pockets on to the front of the T-shirt using big stitches.

③ Use the fabric marker pen to draw the outlines of sweets, coins and dice just above each pocket. Here are ideas for other items you could draw – pencils, rubbers, jewellery, sunglasses, favourite toys, lipstick and hair clips.

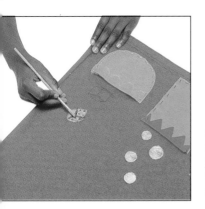

HANDY HINT

Place a piece of card inside the body of the T-shirt when sewing on the pockets. This will stop you from accidentally sewing the front and the back of the T-shirt together.

④ Insert a piece of card into the body of the T-shirt. Paint the sweet wrappers and dice in bright colours. Use gold fabric paint for the coins. When the paint is dry, put on your T-shirt and fill the pockets with all your treasures!

Modern Artist

Modern art has never been so much fun or so easy. To make this colourful, paint splattered T-shirt, you just have to flick a paintbrush loaded with runny fabric paint all over the T-shirt. Try not to splatter paint over walls, furniture and members of your family – it could mean the early end to a promising artistic career!

YOU WILL NEED
Newspaper
Large sheet of card
Short sleeved T-shirt
Pot of water
*Fabric paint (yellow, orange,
    red, green, blue)*
Thick paintbrush

1 Cover the work surface with newspaper. Insert pieces of card inside the body and sleeves of the T-shirt. Add water to the fabric paints to make them runny. Dip the thick brush into the yellow fabric paint and flick it at the T-shirt.

2 Wash the brush thoroughly before changing colours. Dip the clean brush into the orange fabric paint and flick the brush at the T-shirt.

3 Do the same with the red, green and blue fabric paints. You can flick more colours if you like. Allow the paint to dry before wearing your T-shirt.

HANDY HINT

When splatter painting, start with the lightest colour and then apply the darker colours. The last colour that you splatter on to the T-shirt should be the darkest.

To make a finer splatter, drag a plastic ruler across the bristles of a nail brush that has been dipped in fabric paint. Always pull the ruler toward you, unless you want to splatter yourself!

Disco Dazzler

Wear this wild T-shirt to be the centre of attention. The patterns will positively glow in the dark under ultra-violet light. This is because they have been painted using fluorescent fabric paint. To be the ultimate Disco Dazzler, paint the names of your favourite bands on to the back of the T-shirt.

YOU WILL NEED
Large sheet of card
Short sleeved black T-shirt
Chalk fabric marker
Pot of water
Medium paintbrush

Fluorescent fabric paint
(yellow, blue, pink,
orange, green)
Puffa fabric paint (orange,
yellow, purple, red)
Hairdryer

1 Insert pieces of card inside the body and sleeves of the T-shirt. Use the chalk fabric marker to draw the outlines of triangles, spirals and zigzag patterns all over the front and the sleeves of the T-shirt.

2 Use fluorescent yellow, blue, pink, orange and green fabric paint to fill in the outlines. To make other colours, simply mix different colours together. Allow the fabric paint to dry.

3 Decorate the T-shirt with dots and squiggles of orange, yellow, purple and red puffa paint. To make the puffa fabric paint puff up, dry it with a hairdryer. Set the hairdryer to its coolest setting.

4 Decorate the bottom of the T-shirt with a zigzag pattern using puffa fabric paint. Once again, use the hairdryer set to its coolest temperature to dry the puffa paint.

Hair-do Suzie

How will you do Suzie's hair today? Will it be in plaits, ponytails or hanging loose? You could even do her hair in lots of fine braids with beads threaded on to the ends! Instead of hair clips, tie Suzie's hair with brightly coloured ribbons.

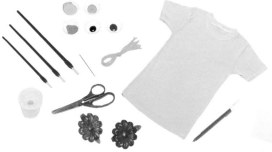

YOU WILL NEED

Large sheet of card
Short sleeved T-shirt
Fabric marker pen
Pot of water
Fine, medium and thick
    paintbrushes

Fabric paint (light pink,
    dark pink, white, red,
    blue, black)
Scissors
Yellow knitting wool
Embroidery needle
2 hair clips

1 Insert a piece of card inside the body of the T-shirt. Use the fabric marker pen to draw the outline of the face and neck on to the T-shirt. Hair-do Suzie's head needs to be about 15cm long.

2 Use the thick brush to fill in the outline with light pink fabric paint. Use the dark pink to make Suzie's rosy cheeks. Allow the paint to dry thoroughly before starting the next step.

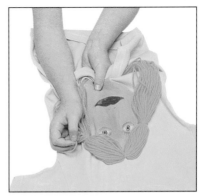

③ Draw the eyes, nose and lips with the fabric marker pen. Use the medium brush to paint the eyes white and the lips red. When dry, use the fine brush to paint the irises blue and then the pupils and eyelashes with black fabric paint.

④ To make the hair, you will need 40 strands of knitting wool, each 60cm long. Lay out the strands so the ends are even. Tie them together at the middle with a piece of wool.

⑤ Thread the embroidery needle with a long length of knitting wool and knot the end. Place the hair on to the head. Sew it on to the T-shirt with stitches at the top and at the sides. Tie the hair into two ponytails with the hair clips.

HANDY HINT

To keep Hair-do Suzie's golden locks in good condition, this T-shirt should be handwashed and laid out flat to dry. Do not forget to remove hair clips and ribbons before washing the T-shirt.

Busy Executive

When is a T-shirt not a T-shirt? When it is painted to look like an executive's shirt and tie. Dressing up a plain T-shirt to look like something else is easy. You could paint a police officer's jacket and include details like the badge, whistle and radio, or a doctor's coat complete with stethoscope. There is no end to the mischief your disguises could cause!

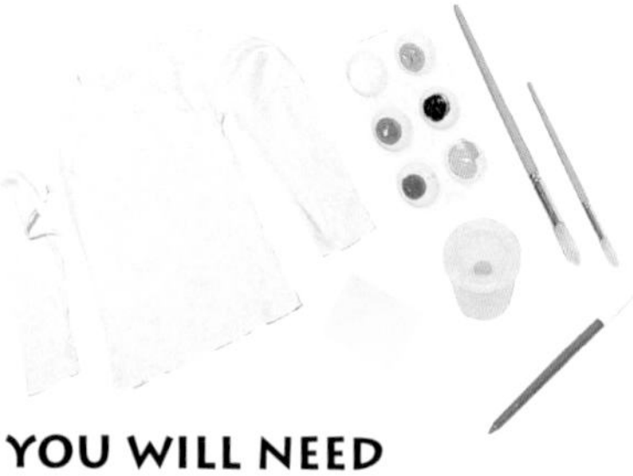

YOU WILL NEED

Large sheet of card
Long sleeved T-shirt
Fabric marker pen
Pot of water
Fabric paint (pale blue, black, orange,
  red, white, gold)
Fine and medium paintbrushes

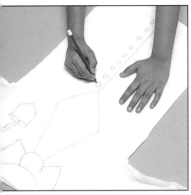

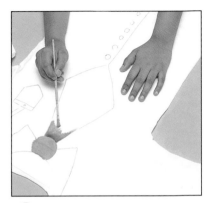

1 Insert pieces of card inside the body and sleeves of the T-shirt. Use the fabric marker pen to draw the outlines of the collar, shirt front, tie and pocket on the front of the T-shirt. Draw a watch on to one sleeve.

2 Paint the tie with pale blue fabric paint using the medium brush. Use a darker shade of blue under the knot of the tie so that it stands out. When dry, decorate the tie with dots of orange fabric paint.

3 Paint the buttons and shirt front dark blue. Use a lighter blue for the collar and pocket. Allow to dry before painting dark blue stripes on to the collar and pocket. Paint a button on to the pocket.

4 Mix white and black fabric paint to make grey. Paint the watch face grey. When dry, paint the red outline and black hands. To make the watch look valuable, paint the watchband with gold fabric paint. Allow to dry.

5 Turn the T-shirt over, making sure that the pieces of card are still in place. Use the fabric marker pen to draw the outline of the collar on to the back of the T-shirt. Paint the collar as before. To finish, draw and paint the rest of the watchband.

HANDY HINT
Copy pictures of business people, police officers and doctors from magazines so that your T-shirt design is really accurate. Colour pictures will make it easy for you to choose exactly the right colours.

45

Noughts and Crosses

This T-shirt is great fun. Well, it is not often that an item of clothing doubles-up as a board game, is it? Wear it when you are travelling long distances and you will never be bored. Before washing the T-shirt, remove the noughts and crosses.

YOU WILL NEED

2 sheets of card
Short sleeved T-shirt
Ruler
Fabric marker pen
Pearl fabric paint
  (orange)
Pencil

Tracing paper
Paper
Scissors
Blue and red felt
Fabric glue and brush
9 sticky back hook and
  loop dots

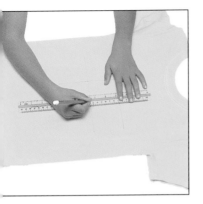

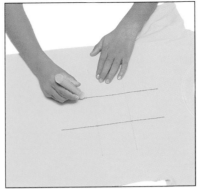

1 Insert a piece of card inside the body of the T-shirt. Use a ruler and fabric marker pen to measure and draw the Noughts and Crosses grid. The lines should be 24cm long and 8cm apart.

2 Go over the lines with orange pearl fabric paint in a squeezy tube. Move the tube evenly along the lines – otherwise the pearl paint will form blobs. Allow the pearl paint to dry thoroughly.

3 To make the Noughts and Crosses templates, see page 11. Place the templates on to the felt and draw around them. You will need four red noughts and four blue crosses. Cut out the shapes. Also cut out four small blue ovals and glue these on to the noughts with fabric glue.

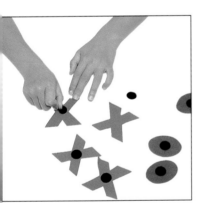

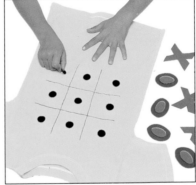

4 Remove the backing from one side of a hook and loop dot. Press the sticky surface on to the back of one of the felt shapes. Repeat for all the shapes.

5 Remove the backing from the remaining dots and press these into the centre of each square on the grid. You are now ready to play Noughts and Crosses!

Pizza Pizzazz

This T-shirt is the ultimate in take-away food. Wherever you go, you take the pizza with you! This mushroom and tomato pizza is just the first course. Why not make a cheese and ham pizza as well!

YOU WILL NEED
2 sheets of card
Short sleeved T-shirt
Plate
Fabric marker pen
Pot of water
Fabric paint (red)
Thick paintbrush
Pearl fabric paint (gold)
Pencil
Tracing paper
Scissors
Brown, light brown and red felt
Fabric glue and brush
10 sticky back hook and loop dots

1 Insert a piece of card inside the body of the T-shirt. Place a medium size plate in the centre of the T-shirt and draw around it with the fabric marker pen. This is the base of the pizza.

2 Use the thick brush to cover the pizza base with a tomato red fabric paint. Allow this to dry before painting the crispy crust with gold pearl paint. This pizza is looking very delicious!

3 Make the templates for the mushrooms and the tomatoes on page 12. Place the mushroom template on to the felt and draw around it. You will need to draw five whole brown mushrooms and five pale brown mushroom tops. Cut out the pieces. Glue the mushroom tops on to the whole mushrooms with fabric glue.

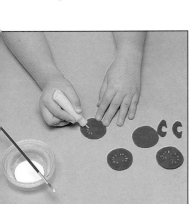

4 Draw around the tomato template on red felt. You will need five whole tomatoes and ten tomato segments. Cut out the pieces. Glue the segments on to the whole tomatoes with fabric glue. Paint the seeds using the gold pearl paint.

5 Remove the backing from the hook and loop dots. Press five loop-sided dots around the edge of the pizza. Press hook-sided dots on to the back of the mushrooms and tomatoes. What would you like – a mushroom pizza or a tomato pizza?

HANDY HINT

If you cannot find hook and loop dots with self-adhesive backing, you can use fabric glue to stick the dots to the T-shirt and to the felt shapes. Remove the felt shapes before washing this T-shirt.

Really Wild

It is time to go on safari, but you must tread softly so that the real Kings of the Jungle do not see you! Majestic lions and ferocious tigers may not like human impersonators prowling on their territory.

YOU WILL NEED
Large sheet of card
Long sleeved T-shirt
Fabric marker pen
Pot of water
Fabric paint (brown, red,
orange, yellow, black)
Thick paintbrush

1 Insert a piece of card inside the body of the T-shirt. Use the fabric marker pen to draw the outlines of the tiger stripes on to the front of the T-shirt.

2 Paint the stripes using brown, red, orange, yellow and black fabric paints. It does not matter if the stripes are uneven as this will make them look more realistic.

3 When the paint is dry, turn the T-shirt over. Check that the card is still in place. Use the marker pen to draw more stripes and a tail on to the back of the T-shirt.

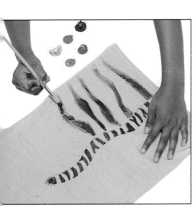

4 Use the same colours as before to paint the stripes and tail. Allow your Really Wild T-shirt to dry before you start prowling and growling in it.

Glitzy Stars

This twinkling T-shirt is perfect for a party or special occasion. The glitter and sequins will make the stars sparkle under lights. Fabric glitter is specially made for use on fabrics. It can be bought in hobby and craft shops. Ordinary craft glitter should not be used for this design.

YOU WILL NEED

Large sheet of card
Short sleeved T-shirt
Fabric marker pen
Pot of water
Fabric paint (blue, yellow, white, red, pink, green)
Fine paintbrush
Pearl fabric paint (yellow)
Glitter fabric paint (gold)
Fabric glue and brush
Fabric glitter
Sequins
Sheet of paper

1 Insert a piece of card inside the body of the T-shirt. Use the fabric marker pen to draw the outlines of stars all over the front of the T-shirt.

2 Use the fine brush to paint the stars with blue, green, red, yellow and pink fabric paints. To make lighter shades of these colours, add white.

3 Paint around the edges of the stars with yellow pearl fabric paint and gold glitter fabric paint. Decorate the stars with dots and spots of yellow and gold.

4 Now it is time to really add some sparkle to this T-shirt. Paint the stars with fabric glue. While the glue is still wet, sprinkle on fabric glitter and sequins. Allow the glue to dry.

5 To remove excess fabric glitter and sequins, gently shake the T-shirt over a piece of paper. Carefully fold the paper to form a spout and pour the fabric glitter and sequins back into their containers.

All-weather T-shirt

This T-shirt can be designed to match any weather forecast. That is why it is called the All-weather T-shirt. If rain is coming, then paint a rainbow on the back and flashes of lightning on the front. The perfect winter T-shirt could be covered with snowflakes.

YOU WILL NEED
Large piece of card
Long sleeved, light blue T-shirt
Plate
Fabric marker pen
Pot of water
Fabric paint (yellow, red, white
Medium and thick paintbrushe.
Sponge

HANDY HINT
To make the clouds light and wispy, do not load too much paint on to the sponge. To print the interesting texture of the sponge, press the sponge gently on to the T-shirt.

54

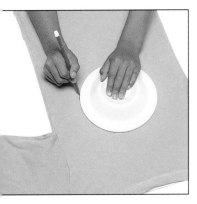

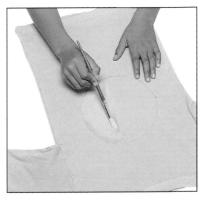

1 Insert pieces of card inside the body and sleeves of the T-shirt. Use the fabric marker pen to draw around a medium size plate on to the back of the T-shirt.

2 Paint the circle with a sunny yellow fabric paint. Do this with the thick brush. Allow to dry. Use the marker pen to give the Sun a smiling face and lots of rays.

3 Mix red and yellow fabric paints to make shades of orange. Use this to paint the eyes, mouth and rays.

4 When the fabric paint is dry, turn the T-shirt over. Check that the pieces of card are still in place. Lightly dip the dry sponge into white fabric paint.

5 Dab the sponge on to the front of the T-shirt to make a wispy cloud. Repeat until the front of the T-shirt and sleeves are covered. Allow the paint to dry.

Birthday Present

Why not make this T-shirt as a gift for a friend's birthday? They could wear it to their own party! It is important that the painted ribbon is identical to the real ribbon. To achieve this, you may have to mix fabric paints together to make exactly the right colour.

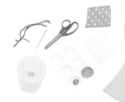

YOU WILL NEED

Large sheet of card
Short sleeved T-shirt
Ruler
Fabric marker pen
Pot of water
Fabric paint (green, white, pink)

Medium and thick paintbrushes
40-50cm of wide, green ribbon
Scissors
Green sewing thread
Sewing needle

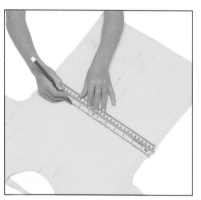

1 Insert pieces of card inside the body and sleeves of the T-shirt. Use the ruler and fabric marker pen to draw two parallel lines down the centre of the T-shirt and two parallel lines across the T-shirt, as shown.

2 Paint the area inside the lines with green fabric paint. Do this with the thick brush. These are the ribbons on the present. Make the edges of the ribbon as straight as possible. Allow to dry.

3 Use the medium brush to decorate the painted ribbon with small dots of white fabric paint. Wash the brush. Cover the rest of the T-shirt with larger pink dots. Allow to dry.

4 Tie the length of ribbon into a big bow. Trim the ends. Thread the needle with thread and tie a knot in the end. Position the bow where the painted ribbons cross and sew it into place. Keep sewing until the bow is securely fixed.

HANDY HINT

Try adding a little water to a fabric paint – it makes the paint easier to apply and changes the colour slightly. The more water you add, the lighter the colour will become. Do not make the fabric paint too runny or it will drip all over the place.

57

Hungry Cat

This Hungry Cat is dreaming of a seafood feast. If the dream does not come true, the cat's contented purr will become a moaning miaow. Does the cat get its wish? Look at the back of the T-shirt to find out. Oh dear, poor little fish!

YOU WILL NEED

2 sheets of card
Pencil
Tracing paper
Scissors
Short sleeved T-shirt
Fabric marker pen
Pot of water
Fabric paint (blue, white, black, red,
  yellow, orange, pink)
Medium and thick paintbrushes
Sponge
Black embroidery thread
Embroidery needle

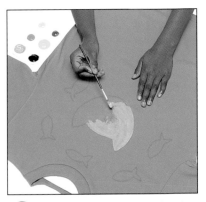

1 Insert a piece of card inside the body of the T-shirt. Make the cat template on page 12. Place the template on to the front of the T-shirt and draw around it with the fabric marker pen.

2 Use the thick brush to paint the cat's face with blue-grey fabric paint. To make this colour, mix blue, white and black fabric paints. Add more white to this colour to paint the cat's markings.

3 Draw five fish using the fabric marker pen. Paint the fish different colours. This hungry cat is dreaming of its fishy lunch, so give it a happy and contented face. Paint and decorate the cat's fancy collar.

4 Make the stencil for the fish skeleton on page 13. When the fabric paint is dry, turn the T-shirt over. Place the stencil on to the back of the T-shirt and dab it with a sponge dipped in red fabric paint. Lift off the stencil. Stencil four more skeletons in different colours.

5 When the fabric paint is dry, remove the card and turn the T-shirt over again. Thread the needle with black embroidery thread and tie a knot at the end. Sew four long stitches on either side of the cat's nose to make the whiskers.

Optical Illusion

If you look at this crazy Optical Illusion for too long you are bound to feel dizzy. There was a Dutch artist called Escher who became very famous for his paintings of bizarre optical illusions. In his paintings, nothing was ever as it should be – water flowed uphill and a school of fish would become a flock of birds before your eyes.

YOU WILL NEED
Large sheet of card
Short sleeved T-shirt
Fabric marker pen
Pearl fabric paint (black)

1 Insert a piece of card inside the body of the T-shirt. Use the fabric marker pen to draw a large rectangle on to the front of the T-shirt. Draw more rectangles getting smaller and smaller inside the large rectangle.

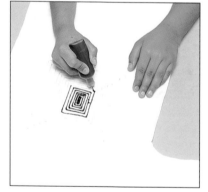

2 Go over the design with black pearl fabric paint in a squeezy container. If you are using a new container of pearl fabric paint, cut the nozzle close to the top. This will make it easy to paint fine lines.

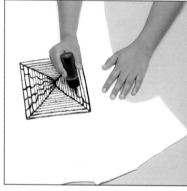

3 Paint lines with the black pearl fabric paint from each corner to the middle. This will divide the rectangle into four triangles. Then paint wiggly lines in the two side triangles with the black paint.

4 Divide each line in the bottom triangle into rectangles using the black pearl paint. The rectangles will get smaller as they get closer to the centre. To finish off your Optical Illusion, paint alternate rectangles black to make a checkered pattern.

HANDY HINT

This design is quite complicated, so it might be a good idea to practise it on a piece of paper. When you feel confident, draw the design on to the T-shirt. To make straight lines, you can use a ruler.

Sunny Sunflower

On the Sunny Sunflower T-shirt you can show off all your artistic flair for colour, texture and shape. In fact, your painting will be so good that it will be framed in gold. There is only one thing missing from this painting – the signature of the talented artist.

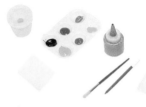

YOU WILL NEED

Large sheet of card
Short sleeved T-shirt
Fabric marker pen
Pot of water
Medium paintbrush

Fabric paint (black, yellow, red, orange, light blue, gold)
Glitter fabric paint (gold)

1 Insert a piece of card inside the body of the T-shirt. Use the fabric marker pen to draw the outline of the sunflower and the fancy picture frame.

2 Paint the centre of the sunflower with black fabric paint. Use shades of yellow, red and orange to paint the petals. Allow the paint to dry.

3 Use a sky blue fabric paint for the background of your sunflower painting. Take care not to paint over the petals or into the frame. Allow the paint to dry.

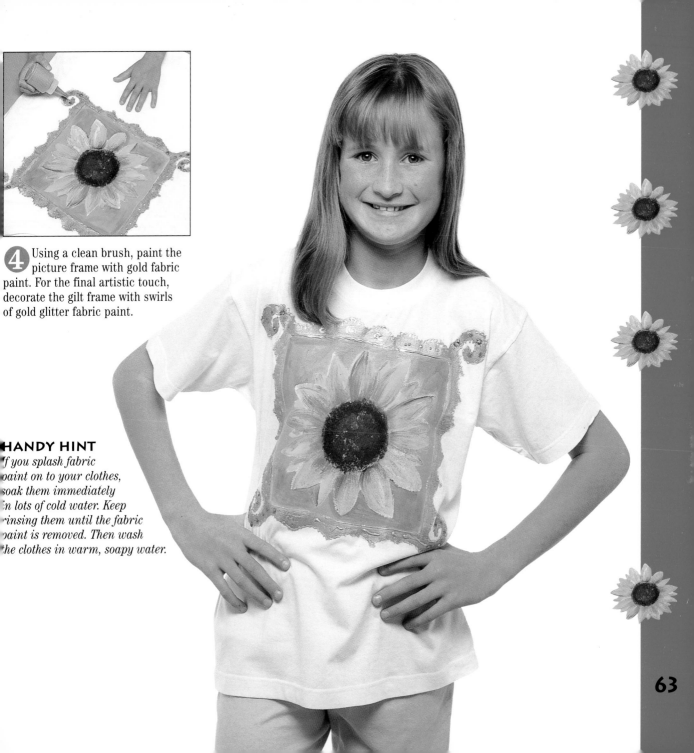

4 Using a clean brush, paint the picture frame with gold fabric paint. For the final artistic touch, decorate the gilt frame with swirls of gold glitter fabric paint.

HANDY HINT
If you splash fabric paint on to your clothes, soak them immediately in lots of cold water. Keep rinsing them until the fabric paint is removed. Then wash the clothes in warm, soapy water.

ACKNOWLEDGEMENTS

The Publishers would like to thank the following children for modelling for this book –

Nana Addae

Kristina Chase

Charlie Coulson

Reece Johnson

Alex Lindblom-Smith

Sophie Lindblom-Smith

Imran Miah

Lucy Nightingale

Tom Swaine Jameson

Sophie Viner

Gratitude also to their parents and Walnut Tree Walk Primary School.

For information about fabric painting and equipment, contact the Dylon Consumer Advice Line on the following telephone numbers – 0181 663 4296 (UK), 1800 025 021 (Aust.) or 001 864 576 5050 (USA).

This book is dedicated to Lucy.